44 SELECTED DUETS

FOR TWO FLUTES

(Easy – Intermediate)

Compiled and Edited by

JAY ARNOLD

We take pride in presenting in this book the works of four great masters in composing and arranging music for the flute in duet form. The duets selected will appeal to the early grade player, advancing to the intermediate stage. Ensemble experience is of much importance in bringing out tone quality, technique and an exchange of ideas in musical approach and interpretation by the performers. It is assumed, of course, that each player will master the selected part in solo form before combining the performance with the other part.

CONTENTS

© Copyright MCMLXXIII by Edward Schuberth & Co., Inc.
263 Veterans Boulevard, Carlstadt, N.J. 07072
International Copyright Secured   Made in U.S.A.

TWENTY-FIVE EASY DUETS

Opus 55, Book 1

ERNESTO KOEHLER
(1849-1907)

Allegro moderato (Kreutzer)

amoroso

7

Poco sostenuto (Mendelssohn)

marziale

p

8

allargando

a tempo

Marziale

12

stentate   a tempo

f

Allegro moderato (Boieldieu)

14

Moderato (Keyll)

15

Marziale

16

Allegretto

17

Allegro moderato (Mozart)

18

Moderato (Donizetti)

19

doloroso

Allegro (Mozart)

20

Moderato

21

Allegretto grazioso

23

Largo (Bellini)

24

Mazurka (Chopin)

25

TWELVE DUETS

HEINRICH SOUSSMANN
(1796-1848)

Fine

Da Capo al Fine

38

Allegretto M.M. ♩ = 84

staccato   *f*

f staccato

6

Allegro M.M. ♩ = 126

10

D.C. al Fine
senza replica

Allegretto M.M. ♩ = 100

12

FOUR DUETS
From Opus 51, Book 1

LUIGI HUGUES
(1836-1913)

Allegretto moderato ♩ = 96

2

Andante mosso ♩= 96

3

dolce con espressione

THREE DUETS
Opus 27

CARL STAMITZ
(1746-1801)

Romance

Un poco presto

Menuetto

Trio

dolce

Fine

Menuett D.C. al Fine

Romance

Fugato
Allegro

INVENTION

(In F)

JOHANN SEBASTIAN BACH

TOCCATA AND FUGUE
(In D Minor)

JOHANN SEBASTIAN BACH

Fugue

Allegro con moto

MUSETTE

Giocoso

JOHANN SEBASTIAN BACH

JESU, JOY OF MAN'S DESIRING

JOHANN SEBASTIAN BACH

AVE MARIA

JOHANN SEBASTIAN BACH

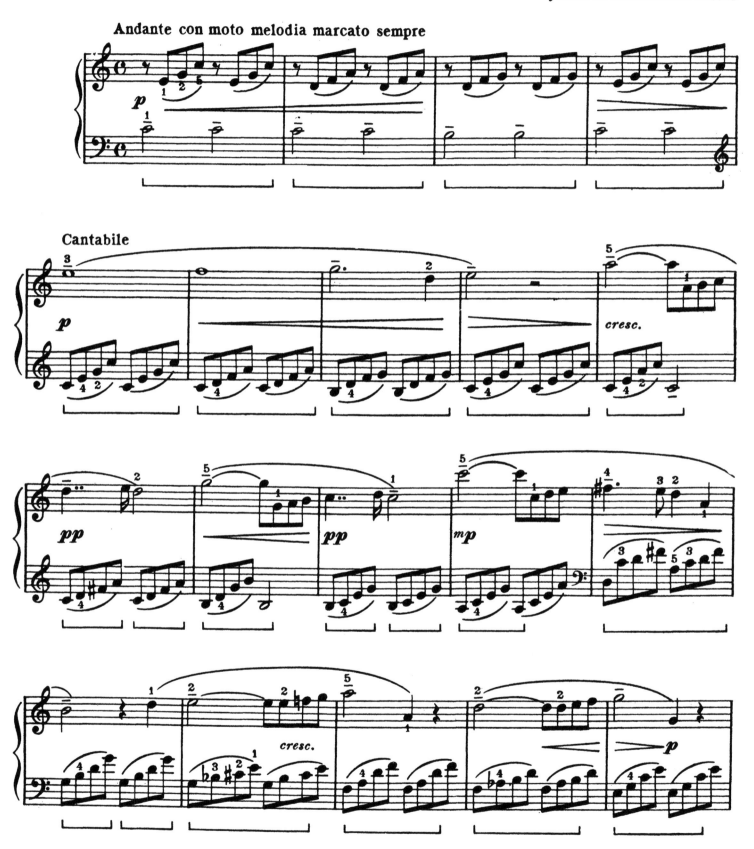

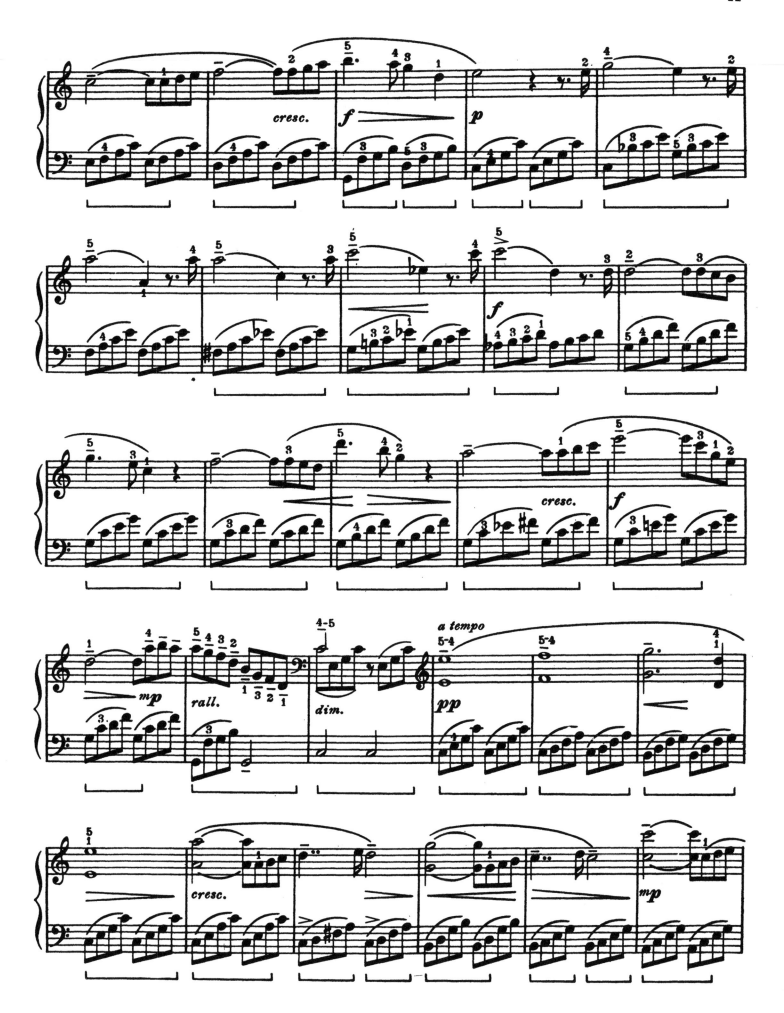

MINUET

(FROM THE NOTEBOOK OF ANNA MAGDALENA BACH)

JOHANN SEBASTIAN BACH

Allegretto grazioso

CONCERTO ITALIANA

JOHANN SEBASTIAN BACH

II.

FUGUE
(IN C MAJOR)

PRELUDE
(IN C MINOR)

Allegro vivace

FUGUE
(IN D MINOR)

PRELUDE
(IN E MINOR)

Allegro molto moderato

FUGUE
(IN E MINOR)

PRELUDE
IN F

FUGUE

PRELUDE
(IN G)

FUGUE

Allegretto vivace

PRELUDE
(IN A FLAT)

Moderato

FUGUE
(IN A FLAT)

FANTASIA CHROMATICA

JOHANN SEBASTIAN BACH

Allegro impetuoso

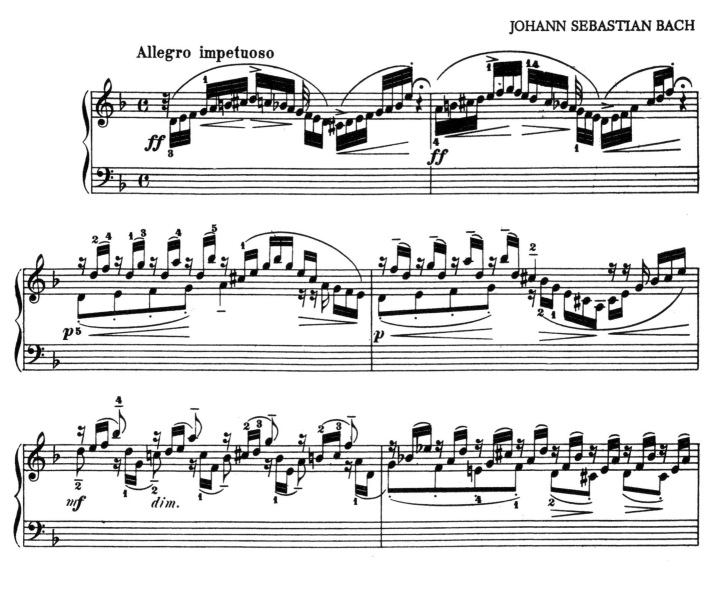

il Basso sempre un poco tenuto

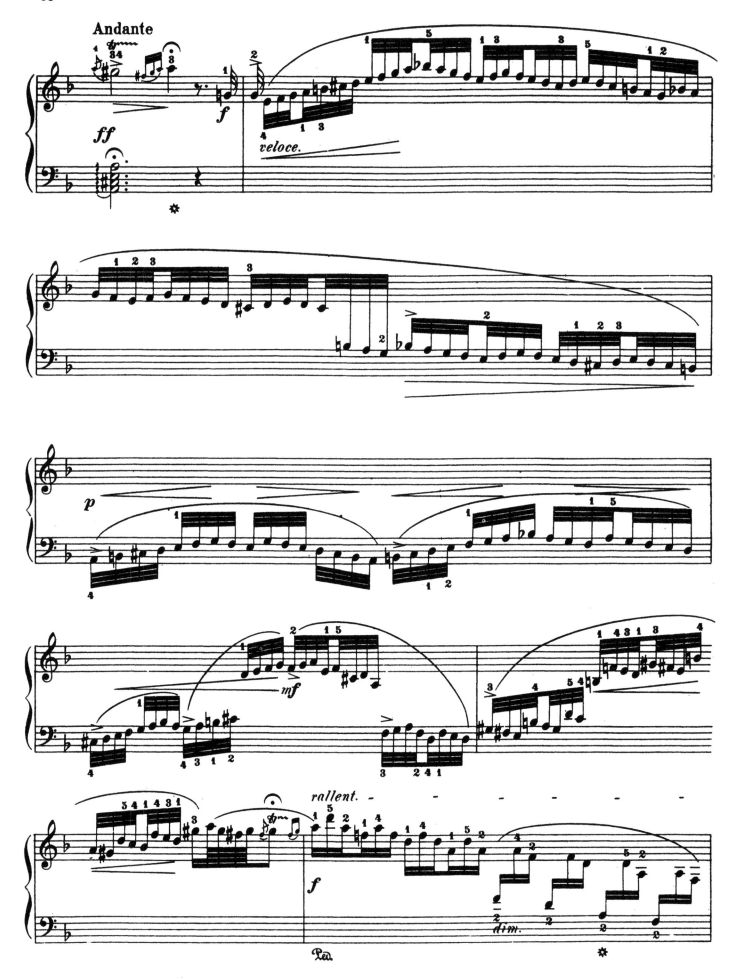

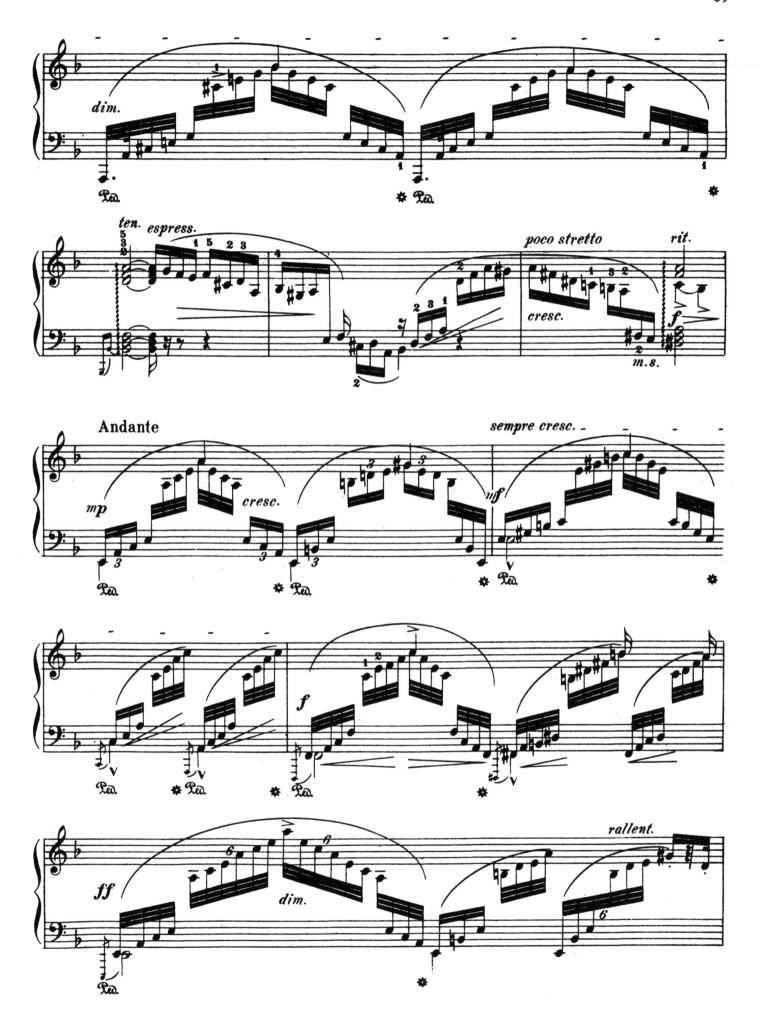

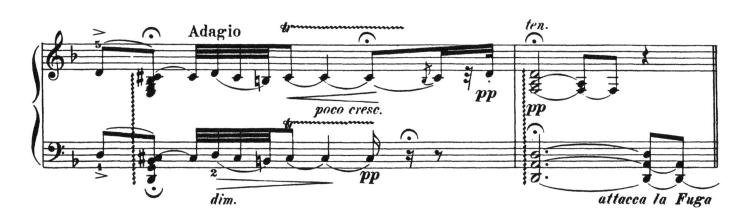

Fuga

Poco Allegro e tranquillo

Poco a poco animando il tempo sin' al Fine

PASSEPIED

JOHANN SEBASTIAN BACH

Trio
Meno vivace

Fine

Passepied da capo

SARABANDE

(In A Minor)

JOHANN SEBASTIAN BACH

ALLEMANDE

Allegro moderato

INVENTION
(IN F MINOR)

Andante espressivo

INVENTION
(IN B MINOR)

Allegro moderato

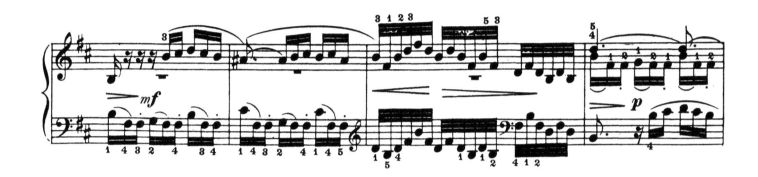

FUGUE IN A MINOR

This Fugue is well adapted for public performance, being brilliant, showy and effective, and it was formerly played by Liszt in his Concerts. It is also exceedingly useful as an exercise in developing strength and flexibility of finger.

JOHANN SEBASTIAN BACH

a) A short trill concluding without a turn, *(Nachschlag.)* in order that the proper Metre or Rhythmic form of the dotted note thus; may be observed.

a) A very short trill concluding without a turn. (*Nachschlag*) in order that the proper Metre or Rhythmic form of the dotted note thus; may be observed.

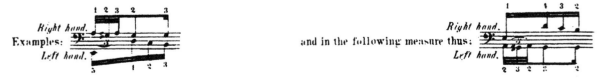

a) In old editions the sign of embellishment used in this measure is the same in both instances, viz: the inverted Mordent. (*Pralltriller*) thus, ⁕; and the manner of playing is, therefore, as follows:

According to the rule generally observed in Bach's time the first sign should be simply a Mordent (not inverted) thus, ⁕, in which case the manner of playing would be as follows; etc.

a) A short trill beginning with the principal tone, on account of the melodic effect, and ending with a turn. as follows;

MINUET IN B FLAT

JOHANN SEBASTIAN BACH

Moderato

SARABANDE
(In E Minor)

JOHANN SEBASTIAN BACH

Andante espressivo

POLONAISE
(IN G MINOR)
No. 1

JOHANN SEBASTIAN BACH

Moderato

GAVOTTE

(In D Minor)

JOHANN SEBASTIAN BACH

Moderato

Original: a)

GAVOTTE
(In D)

JOHANN SEBASTIAN BACH

AIR WITH VARIATIONS

JOHANN SEBASTIAN BACH

Var. 2

Var.3

Var.4

Var. 5

Var. 6

Var. 7

136

MENUET
(FROM "PARTITA I")

Allegretto animato
sempre legato

D. C. al Fine.

MARCH

POLONAISE (G Minor - No. 2)

POLONAISE
(IN E)

GIGUE
No. 1

GIGUE
No. 2

Molto Allegro

LOURE

GIGUE (No. 3)

CONCLUDED - NEXT PAGE

FRENCH SUITE (IN "E") - Excerpt

Allegro moderato

COURANTE

Allegro e leggiero

SARABANDE (in E)

WACHET AUF

Chorale Prelude

Wa - chet auf ruft uns die Stim - me.

FANTASIA IN C MINOR

JOHANN SEBASTIAN BACH

Maestoso patetico

a) As the triplet-rhythm predominates, all the ornaments must, consequently, be divided in accordance with it.

b)

C) Trill in triplets, as at **b**)

PRELUDE AND FUGUE

(In A Minor)

JOHANN SEBASTIAN BACH

PRELUDE
(IN "D")

FUGUE
(IN "D")

TWO MINUETS

Menuett I
Andantino con grazia

JOHANN SEBASTIAN BACH

Menuett II

CAPRICCIO

(The Journey)

Die Abreise

1. Die Freunde bitten: „Bleibe bei uns.“

The Departure

1. The friends plead: "Remain with us."

JOHANN SEBASTIAN BACH

2. Man schildert die Gefahren der Fremde. | 2. They describe the dangers in foreign lands.

3. Trauern und Klagen | 3. Sorrow and regret

Adagio molto

4. Abschiednehmen | 4. Farewell

5. Der Postillion kommt | 5. The postillion comes

6. Glückliche Fahrt | 6. Pleasant journey
Fuga all' imitazione della cornetta di Postiglione

BOURREE
(No. 2)

JOHANN SEBASTIAN BACH

Allegro